C H O S I N
RESERVOIR

CHOSIN RESERVOIR

As I Remember Koto-ri Pass, North Korea,
December 1950

MEMOIRS OF MERRILL HARPER, LT. COL. US ARMY (RETIRED) CIRCA 1948–1970

As narrated to and compiled by David A. Givan
Foreword by David A. Givan

iUniverse, Inc.
Bloomington

CHOSIN RESERVOIR
As I Remember Koto-ri Pass, North Korea, December 1950

iUniverse books may be ordered through booksellers or by contacting:

iUniverse
1663 Liberty Drive
Bloomington, IN 47403
www.iuniverse.com
1-800-Authors (1-800-288-4677)

ISBN: 978-1-4697-8956-9 (sc)
ISBN: 978-1-4697-8959-0 (hc)
ISBN: 978-1-4697-8957-6 (ebk)

Printed in the United States of America

iUniverse rev. date: 06/05/2012

Dedicated to my wife, Jule, our daughter, Julie, and our son John.
Jule and I were married fifty-five years.

Figure 1 Jule Harper

Our daughter, Julie, was a fighter. Unlike me, Julie fought no battles in foreign countries. Nor were there intervals of peace in the savage battle she did participate in. There were times of remission. Never a cease-fire. She continuously, courageously, and cheerfully fought an opponent within her own body for fifteen years. Ultimately that enemy, ovarian cancer, did devastate her body—but not her spirit. She lived from 1959 until 2010.

Figure 2 Julie Harper

This is my son John and I at the Korean War Memorial in Colorado Springs, Colorado. John has been very instrumental in the publishing of my book and has been helping me out in my day to day activities. Since it is just John and I left, we try to spend as much time together as possible, either eating out or enjoying a nice ride on a Sunday afternoon in the mountains.

Figure 3 Merrill and son, John Harper

And when ye shall hear of wars and rumours of wars, be ye not troubled: for such things must needs be; but the end shall not be yet. For nation shall rise against nation, and kingdom against kingdom: and there shall be earthquakes in diverse places, and there shall be famines and troubles: these are the beginnings of sorrows.

—Mark 13:7–8
(King James version of the Holy Bible)

CONTENTS

FOREWORD

By David A. Givan

Merrill's memoirs were related to me with that vividness that is born simultaneously as personal experiences emerge. Conveyance of facts about those experiences that are by turns heartbreaking, astounding, enlightening, frightening, awesome, or embarrassing is a task he has now embraced. Occasionally these accounts reveal touching emotions. At other times Merrill embellished his recollections with priceless humor. But how many ways are there to mitigate the grisly truths that must emerge when a combat veteran honestly describes the real-life battlefields he was on?

Pictures of battlefields in Korea and elsewhere often portray horrendous destruction and carnage. Battlefields as experienced by those who fought there do not exclude common enemies such as frigid weather, snow, drenching rains, tropical heat, hostile terrain, snakes, etc. All who are there, foe or friend, may be subject to such conditions. Beyond the gamut of adverse situations to be encountered, human survival is threatened by devastating man-made weapons, concoctions, equipment, devices, and contraptions that may be introduced by both friend and foe.

In spite of, or more correctly, because of the massacre, a given battleground hosts courage, cowardice, honor, shame, love, and hate. Wise decisions and devastating mistakes emerge. If there are survivors from such a battleground, those survivors have stories they may or may not tell. Merrill is such a survivor. He has chosen to orally relate some of his stories to me. With the aid of a tape recorder and word processor I have captured and endeavored to preserve in writing those incidents he chose to describe. My goal, simply stated, is to compile Merrill's memoirs so as to formulate a factual, chronological narrative that beckons your attention.

Since Merrill is an enthusiastic and gifted storyteller and he is relating personal experiences, pertinent facts and credible dialogue emerge naturally. Not much research and not much creativity was (is) required of me. However, I did do research in quest of maps, pictures, and document excerpts from other sources in order to benefit from some comparisons, visual portrayals, references, and authentication.

Because this account will be available in electronic as well as printed book form and since text in some areas relates to text in other areas, I have inserted hyperlinks[1] to facilitate finding related information within this document. Hyperlinks may also be used to jump to desired information on a website or to jump from one website to another for related information. If this document is read electronically, placing the cursor on a hyperlink and entering Ctrl+click will access the related information. By using a search engine and following Internet links from website to website, information regarding major US military units seems readily obtainable, with the exception of relatively small units.

---

[1] From hyperlink. (n.d.). *Collins English Dictionary - Complete & Unabridged 10th Edition.* Retrieved February 15, 2012, from Dictionary.com website: http://dictionary.reference.com/browse/hyperlink "A word, phrase, picture, icon, etc, in a computer document on which a user may click to move to another part of the document or to another document."

For example, in a letter to the Korean War Project
(*http://www.koreanwar.org/html/units1/50aaaw.htm*),
Bob Matis wrote the following (text is reproduced exactly):

> It is very hard to find any info for units that were not
> organic to a Division. Such as the 50th AAA Aw Bn
> (SP). which was active at the Inchon Invasion, the
> battle for Seoul, the Iwon Invasion, the drive to the
> Yalu and the help it provided in extracting the marines
> from the Chosin Area.
>
> This unit was attached to the 1st Marine Div., the
> 7th Inf Div., to the 3rd Inf Div., and then finally to
> 8th Army, Yet it is never given mention in any listings
> pertaining to these Divisions.
>
> Stanton in his book titled, "America's Tenth Legion"
> wrote a short paragraph about the great effectiveness
> of the 50ths twin 40 Bofors and the Quad 50 cal. guns
> and their annihilation of the enemy on Hill 1081 at
> Chiphung-ni.
>
> Other than this short paragraph, it is very difficult to
> find any info about the units, battles it served in. The
> Divisions it was attached to, rarely ever mention this
> non-organic unit.
>
> Sincerely,
> Bob Matis

I have an impression that there will be readers who will view
dates and enemy numbers with a degree of skepticism. Other
sources do provide different, less severe numbers and, in some

cases, different dates for specific events. Even though such statistics are less drastic, they do remain formidable. I have recorded the temperatures and enemy numbers as they were perceived and related by Merrill. I make no claim to reconcile all data perfectly, though we have tried. As can be seen from Bob Matis's comments, history of small units' activities is not well documented. Yet, I believe other survivors remain who may provide confirmation for events that are apt to be viewed with awe or skepticism. In fact, I have personally talked with another man who miraculously survived an incident in which wounded soldiers had been stacked like cordwood on army trucks; Merrill estimated one hundred per vehicle. "About ten miles down the road we found the thirty-five 2½-ton trucks with the wounded. The Chinese [had run] a pincer movement, killing the thirty-five drivers and then taking the gas cans, pouring the gas on the wounded, then burning all the wounded alive. [Now] no one was alive." That incident is more fully described subsequently.

I endeavored to eliminate my own comments from the recordings of our conversations whenever possible without making the story less understandable. Phrases such as "Merrill said," "I said," etc., are not used. Instances where my comments or questions are necessary to maintain the integrity of the narrative are printed in italics. Thus, unless the narrative appears in *italics* in the following pages, the words are those Merrill related. Generally, italics will indicate my questions or comments.

PREFACE

by Merrill Harper
Lt. Col. US Army (Retired)
May 2011

US history documents many events about the Korean War, but to my knowledge, none specifically mentions the role of the First Platoon, Battery A, Fiftieth AAA Battalion, X Corps, US Army, in facilitating the withdrawal of the First Marine Division from the Chosin Reservoir.

I was the senior army commander of that platoon. Colonel Lewis E. "Chesty" Puller of the First Marine Division [which was commanded by General O. P. Smith] personally gave me my platoon's first assignments in regard to providing aid for the First Marine Division's escape from the Chinese Army. Here and on the following page I present a thumbnail sketch of my unit's role regarding the First Marine Division and my military training, after which my memoirs are presented in greater detail.

Between 8:00 a.m. and 2:00 p.m. December 15, 1950, we killed about 7,500 Chinese and ran about 2,500 Chinese over the next mountain, all within six hours. For six hours I stood next to my twin 40 mm gun out in the open with my field glasses so that I could see the ten thousand Chinese and direct the fire for my gunner. At 3:00 p.m. on December 15, 1950, I reported to Colonel "Chesty" Puller, marine commander, "Sir, mission completed. The ten thousand Chinese who were in ambush have either been killed or run over to the next mountain."

Colonel Puller looked at me, with my seventeen wounds, and said, "Harper, you have earned the Medal of Honor." Apparently that Medal of Honor has been lost, as well as the other medals he promised.

The weather on Koto-ri Pass was an enemy; the average temperature was minus fifty degrees, and Manchurian winds were ten to forty miles an hour. On the evening of December 14, 1950, two feet of new snow fell, covering the Chinese ambush ten-man foxholes. Koto-ri Pass sits on top of a snowcapped ten-thousand-foot mountain that guards the narrow road from the Chosin Reservoir ten miles to the north and sixty miles to the Sea of Japan.

On December 14, 1950, the battle lines were drawn. The First Marine Division, fifteen thousand men strong, commanded by Major General Oliver Smith, was in a circle on the surface of the Chosin Reservoir's four-foot-thick coating of ice. They were surrounded by three hundred thousand Chinese troops. Ten thousand Chinese troops were deployed on the north side of Koto-ri Pass in ambush position for the marines, while five hundred Chinese troops were on the south side of Koto-ri Pass, also in ambush position.

The marines and my platoon joined forces and dealt with the five hundred Chinese on December 13, 1950. On December 15, the battle in which my platoon played a significant role took place. Total enemy strength was about three hundred ten thousand. US marines' strength was about fifteen thousand. My platoon, US Army, was down to forty men, myself, and my assistant, First Lieutenant Messinger. My platoon was equipped with four twin 40 mm guns, each mounted on a tank chassis. Also, I had three fifty-caliber quad machine guns, each mounted on half-tracks, an armor-plated command vehicle, and one jeep, which only ran in second gear and reverse.

Korean Army history can now be told about Koto-ri Pass, the Chosin Reservoir, and the US Army role in the marines' march to the US Navy Embarkation Center located at Hungnam on the Sea of Japan. I invite you to read all of my memoirs, which follow the next page and cover my entire military career, including assignments in Vietnam and in association with NORAD (North American Aerospace Defense Command) at Cheyenne Mountain, Colorado Springs, Colorado.

Schooling

ROTC, North Georgia College and University, Dahlonega, Georgia, June 5, 1945, to September 20, 1948. Bachelor's degrees: mathematics, physics. Minor: engineering.

Department of Army commissioned me a second lieutenant October 11, 1948; called me to active duty November 30, 1948; and assigned me to the Eighty-Second Airborne, Fort Benning, Georgia, at age nineteen.

1. Basic Officer Artillery School
2. Officer's General Artillery School
3. Air Defense Officer's Training School
4. Officer's School for Non-Judicial Law, Code of Conduct, Military Justice, Geneva Convention
5. Nuclear Weapons Consultant
6. Chemical, Biological, Radiological Consultant
7. Hawk Officer's School
8. Command and General Staff College at Fort Leavenworth, Kansas

NOTE: Senior Instructor, 1957–1959, for sophomore class, two hundred students, at Middle Tennessee University, Murfreesboro, Tennessee. ROTC instructing was seven hours a day.

Figure 4 Merrill Harper 1952

CHAPTER 1

THE MAKING OF A SOLDIER

July 7, 2007

We are gathered together in Falcon,[2] Colorado. It is certainly a beautiful day and we are looking forward to this day.

Well. I'll start at the beginning. I was born in Hartwell,[3] Georgia. I lived six miles west of town and went to school. In junior high I set an all-time school record as [having] the highest rating of any student to graduate. I then went to Hartwell High, where I was among the six highest-ranking students.

From there, I went to college at North Georgia College in Dahlonega, which was a military college where I had ROTC [Reserve Officers Training Corps] and where I got my commission. I started in June of 1945 and graduated in September of 1948, finishing really in under three years of college. I got bachelor's degrees in physics and mathematics, and a minor in engineering.

When I finished college I thought it would be a while before they called me to active duty, but they needed second lieutenants. I was commissioned in October of 1948 and then called to active

---

[2]   Falcon is located in El Paso County, fourteen miles northeast of
       Colorado Springs in Colorado.
[3]   Hartwell is located in Hart County, Georgia.

1

duty November 30, 1948, at Fort Benning,[4] Georgia. There I was initially given the First Platoon of C Company of the 325th Regiment in the Eighty-Second Airborne Division.

They were moving all of their jumpers and troopers to Fort Bragg,[5] North Carolina. I was infantry, so they transferred me to the Third Infantry Division, which at that time was headquartered at Fort Benning. While there I had an infantry platoon.

In early 1949 the Department of Army searched the records of all its second lieutenants. I had the qualifications they were looking for, and they put me in the guided missile program with [Wernher] Von Braun and that group of scientists.[6]

Shortly afterward, in the summer of 1949, I was transferred to El Paso, Texas. Fort Bliss is the station there.[7] When I went out in the heat I never imagined anything to be so hot in my life as crossing Texas and going to El Paso in August.

---

[4] Fort Benning, Georgia is located southeast of Columbus, Georgia.

[5] Fort Bragg is near Fayetteville and Spring Lake, North Carolina.

[6] Search "Operation Paperclip" online for information about this group of German scientists whom the United States recruited after WWII.

[7] Fort Bliss is partly in El Paso County, Texas, and partly in New Mexico, adjacent to the White Sands Missile Range.

CHAPTER 2

THE ASSEMBLY OF MY PLATOON

In June 1950, the Korean War broke out. Three days later they put together the Fiftieth AAA Battalion [Anti Aircraft Artillery Battalion] in which I had the First Platoon, C Battery, Fiftieth AAA Battalion. In three days' time we processed out of Fort Bliss, Texas, and were on a troop train going to Seattle. Before we left, I come to find out my platoon had seven NCOs. I had an assistant lieutenant, and we had thirty-three men who had just come out of the post stockade [*chuckle*]. All my men were felons [*chuckle*], so it was quite a platoon. In Korea we were first attached to X Corps, then to the First Marine Division.

We were assigned to a ninety-day wonder, a West Point lieutenant colonel who had never commanded even a platoon. He'd never left headquarters. Before he was to be promoted to full colonel he had to command the Fiftieth AAA Battalion for ninety days or more. Then he was to be Chief of Staff, Twenty-Fifth Infantry Division, in Korea—a full colonel's position. His West Point contacts must have set it up.

The troop train we rode to Seattle had been in mothballs since World War II. It had about an inch of dust, powder-fine, and the windows were sealed. Going out across New Mexico and

Arizona in that, we went up through Death Valley.[8] It was about 130 degrees in that train, and talk about hot and sweat. There wasn't any way to get away from that heat. We finally broke out in northern California and crossed over into Oregon, and before we got to Portland, I heard the train stoppin'. I asked the conductor what they were doin' and he says it was a minor forestry town where they put water in the train, refilled it. [The train was a steam locomotive.]

So, I got off the train and there was three buildings in the little town. I went into one, and it had a bar and all I wanted was an ice-cold Coca-Cola. I turned around and there was a slot machine, a quarter machine. I had a couple of quarters, so I put a quarter in and money came out. I put another quarter in and money came out. Money came out every time I put in a quarter. I filled up my pockets, and then I tightened my belt as tight as I could get it and I started puttin' quarters around the inside of my shirt. I had my shirt filled up to where it was overflowin' out of the top of my shirt.

'Bout that time I heard the train give the first call, and I put in another quarter and out come more quarters; the next quarter, it stuck inside the machine, and I shook it and I said, "Barkeep, this machine won't play." He said, "You've played enough already. Get out of here!" [*chuckles*] And I tried to run, and I heard the train go second alert, blew the whistle that it was goin'. I couldn't run. I left a trail of quarters all the way across the sandy area toward the train, and I started goin' straight toward the back of the car.

I figured I better take an angle on the train or I'd never make it. The porter, he was wavin'. "Come on! Get in here!" And I started runnin' parallel to the train as best I could, and I got within about three feet; I reached up [but] I couldn't pull myself up, I was so heavy. The porter just literally lifted me right up off the ground,

---

8   Death Valley is a desert valley located in southeastern California.

and quarters went everywhere and I pitched my hat up on the platform, which was full of quarters. I laid there and I was out of breath, and the porter says, "Man, you almost missed this train!" and I says, "I know!" I says, "All those quarters in that hat are yours!" [*chuckles*] So I went inside and I counted the quarters, and I had about ninety-nine dollars in quarters that had survived the trip across the *heh*, sandy area.

CHAPTER 3

BY TRAIN AND SHIP—
SEATTLE TO JAPAN

We went from there into Seattle, and we went by bus onto a little peninsula. There was a little island, like, that had a military post, out in the bay of Seattle. We processed out of there, and every day in July 1950 we got a call to go to the ship. This went on for two weeks, where priority items bumped us off the ship.

We finally got on a ship that had been in mothballs and it too was in not really good condition. We made the great circle route by the Aleutian Islands,[9] goin' down toward the point of Japan. We had orders to land at Pusan,[10] and the Pusan Perimeter[11] had backed up within about thirty miles of Pusan, with all the

---

9   These islands are part of the United States. They make up an archipelago including about three hundred small volcanic islands in the Northern Pacific Ocean. They form an arc between Alaska and the Kamchatka peninsula of Asia.

10   Busan, also known as Pusan. Busan is South Korea's second-largest metropolis, after Seoul.

11   The Pusan Perimeter was the area in southeast Korea that was held by US and South Korean troops in 1950 during the North Korean troops' furthest incursion.

Americans bein' run off the Pusan Perimeter by North Korean troops.

We got just off the northern coast of Japan, and we got hit with a typhoon and the screws on the ship got locked up and we went in a big circle. Every time we'd get broadside, that typhoon would just lift us up and almost turn us over. For three days and three nights, we ran around in a big circle and just about lost our lives before we got there.

But we managed to survive that. We landed at Yokohama,[12] where we went out to the beach and test-fired our weapons. The fishermen had the vessels further down from where we were firing and we could see 'em bringing 'em in. They had these big skids [pallets, eight feet by eight feet], and it looked like four men would bring the skids around to the front and then they'd pull the boat a little further up and then they'd bring the skids back around. In a little bit, I looked around for my men, and none of my men were there. So I walked down to the boat, and on the other side, the people that were carrying these skids were women! And they didn't have anything on from the waist up, and that's where my men were, oglin' these four girls! And so I told one of the men, "Get three of your buddies and pick that thing up." And four GIs could not lift that skid, it was so heavy, and yet those little people could pick 'em up! It was amazing!

That night we went into a bamboo building. Everything was bamboo thatched, and we sat down for supper, and just as I took my first bite, an earthquake of 8.0 hit and my plate went one way and I went the other way. I tried to stand up and I couldn't get up, and finally I ran through the side of the buildin', tryin' to get outside because I didn't want the buildin' to collapse on me. Everybody else made it out, and I tried to grab a tree. Every time I grabbed at that tree, either I moved, or the tree moved. The most

---

[12] Yokohama's port was used as a transshipment base by the United States.

weird feelin' you can ever have is to be in an earthquake of that magnitude. It seemed like it lasted for minutes and minutes, but, actually, it was about twenty seconds.

We had orders to ship out but nobody told us where we were goin', so we went down to the docks and we were loading my equipment. I had four 40 millimeter half-tracks on a tank body, and I had four weapons carriers that had quad machine guns on them, and that's my platoon consisting of four 40 millimeter guns and four fifty-caliber machine guns [40 millimeters = 1.57480 inches, 50 millimeters = 1.96850 inches]. Plus a jeep that only ran in second gear and reverse. Plus a command half-track.

We got to the docks and there was all Japanese stevedores loading the ship. Their first mate says he was gonna put all my machinery down in the hold. I says, "No, you're not! I got orders to test-fire those weapons, and General MacArthur says I'm to be your anti-aircraft defense in case of attack!" He told the captain, and the captain says, "You can only have 'em around the main masts that hold up the riggin' to the top of the ship." And I said, "Go back to him and say, 'No, you can put me, all my guns there, but I'm gonna shoot your riggin' off! 'Cause when we test fire, we're gonna shoot right through your riggin'.'" And he went back to the captain, and that made the captain even madder.

As the first mate and I negotiated our problem, a 48-ton tank was hoisted fifty feet above the dock. All the stevedores began to talk in high-pitched voices. The first mate and I knew something was wrong. The stevedores ran away. So did the first mate and I. Sure enough, the top chain broke and the 48-ton tank fell fifty feet onto the dock, breaking the dock. They towed the 48-ton tank away and started loading again. No one was hurt. So, we finally worked it out to where my guns would be on the ship's outside, to where we'd have a field of fire.

The captain wanted me to sit at his head table, I guess so that he could look me in the eye. Then he told the first mate that my men would not eat with his men. They had drawn good rations. Steak, lobsters, shrimp, you know, for the trip; and I told the first mate, "Well, I'm gonna turn the captain in." He says, "No! Let your men wait till my men finish eating and then your men follow right in behind my men. The captain will never know it." And so I told my men what to do. So we finally got that obstacle resolved. We found out we were gonna land at Inchon, right behind the marines who were goin' in on the beach there, so we first test-fired all our weapons, which worked perfectly, and we were ready.

CHAPTER 4

THE ARMY OF ONE AND THE INCHON INVASION

And so about two o'clock one morning, the first mate wakes me up and says, "Your men have all gone ashore. You need to get up and go. You can go down the rope ladder and you can get into the LST [landing ship transportation] and they'll take you in." So, I had a field jacket, I had my carbine, and I had my pistol, and I had about ten rounds of ammunition and I had a canteen of water but no food. But, unbeknownst to me, the captain had played a trick on me. He sent me in three days in advance of my unit!

So, in the middle of the night we go in between these mud paddies, which I found out later the west coast of Korea has the highest water tides in the world. Thirty-one feet high. So, when the tide goes out there's about ten miles of nothin' but mud and just a little channel, which the LST could negotiate. So we landed with another unit that I'd never seen before and the only thing they had was two other soldiers who got lost from their unit. No food, no water, no nothin'. So for three days and three nights, we kinda held the Inchon landin' by ourselves, as troops came by twenty-four hours a day as they unloaded.

Finally, my unit arrived and I got with them and instead of goin' in with the marines, [following] behind them at Seoul, we had orders to go to Pusan. I was not yet in A Battery of the Fiftieth AAA Battalion. So, it took us two days and two nights of doin' nothin' but driving to get to Pusan.

We went into a staging area which had dikes in it and I still hadn't been assigned a platoon yet and it started raining. Probably an inch an hour—and in about six hours we had two feet of water and everything was under water. So I got me a tarp, put all my clothes and everything on top of it.

About five o'clock next morning the captain wakes up and he says, "Why aren't you out there with your platoon, lookin' after them?" I says, "What platoon?" He says, "I told you last night!" I says, "I'm sorry, sir. I didn't even see you last night." It turns out he had gone (the lieutenant who commanded the first platoon had been promoted to captain from the place I was takin', which was First Platoon, A Battery, Fiftieth AAA Battalion), and they had gone and partied all night.

So, I went out in the rain and the mud and dark, and I was tryin' to find my platoon and nobody would tell me 'cause everybody was so half asleep they didn't wanta get up anyway. So, I finally found my platoon, and all the guns had been taken off the vehicles. I finally found someone, and I said, "What did you do with the guns and the spare parts?" He said, "Oh! It's all down in the mud." They had taken it off in dry weather when we came in the day before. Field-stripped everything, and all of it was layin' on the mud, down under two feet of water.

So I finally got a couple of soldiers and shovels, and we started diggin' out the levee that surrounded us and had the water trapped. We dug and dug. I finally got some more men, and we dug and finally got [an] opening to where the water would empty out. After about two hours of diggin' we managed to break the levee. The water got down to where we could see the parts, and

11

I told 'em: "Make sure you get 'em all wiped down and oiled up before you put 'em in there because we may have to shoot 'em, you know, when we land."

Nobody had had breakfast with all that goin' on, and the captain is gettin' chewed out by the colonel [the ninety-day wonder, the West Point lieutenant colonel who had never commanded even a platoon] because we're not on time to go to the ship to load up, and the captain is chewin' me out every ten minutes and we finally got everything loaded up. We missed the deadline to get to the ship and that didn't make things go over too well.

So we get to the ship, get everybody loaded and the equipment loaded, and the captain informs me I'm the officer of the day for the ship for the next three days and three nights! That meant staying awake in the ship captain's office in case anything had to be taken care of. So, for the next three days and three nights I had to stay awake.

Was this the same captain that you encountered to start with?

Yeah! He was a total drunk. He had brought over about twenty cases of whiskey, and that's all he had in his vehicle was whiskey. And he'd put a bottle in his boot every night before he went to bed, so when he got up he'd take about three or four fingers to get him started and then he'd finish that bottle off during the daytime. Never drew a sober breath. Anyway, I managed to perform my duties as the duty officer.

CHAPTER 5

A HUNDRED TO ONE—
OUTNUMBERED IN HAMHUNG

As we sailed out of Pusan [with new orders] to Iwon [Iwon is about twenty-five miles northeast of Hamhung, North Korea, between Hungnam and Kimch'aek], we were a half-mile from the American cemetery where thousands of our men were buried[13]. One of those men was my college roommate at North Georgia College. He was Charles Worley from Valdosta, Georgia. Charlie was killed on the Pusan Perimeter. His platoon fought the massive North Korean troops. He and his platoon ran out of ammo, so they all died while using their rifles as clubs. Charlie was an ex-marine who survived every marine landing in the South Pacific during World War II. What a friend and a great soldier.

When we got to Iwon (which is also about ninety miles south of Vladivostok, Russia), at that point the waves was comin' in from a storm that was out at sea and we were gettin' waves fifteen to twenty feet high. So when the LSTs pulled in alongside the ship, we had to go down a rope ladder, [then] we had another fifteen feet as it came in to hit the ship. You had to time it so you

---

[13] All bodies buried at the Pusan American cemetery from 1950 to 1953 have been returned to the United States and a cemetery of their family's choice.

went right down into the LST or else you'd go to the bottom of the ocean. It was *really* rough weather. We did'n' lose anybody, but there was some close calls.

We came ashore, and my platoon got assigned to defend X Corps Headquarters[14] at Hamhung, North Korea. The rest of the battalion went into a staging area and did maintenance. We got there, and to further my punishment, my platoon was selected to guard the perimeter, a forty-mile perimeter, with nine vehicles. That was no defense whatsoever, because we had roaming North Korean soldiers coming through the area all the time, and we had to dodge those, so I finally got my men put out in a forty-mile perimeter surrounding X Corps Headquarters.

With that I got battery headquarters to fix a hot meal, and it takes twelve hours to be able to go [deliver all the meals]. Roads were out, ditches, we had to maneuver in and around. And then [at] the same time you had to look out for some enemy troops that was in the area. So every day it was a twelve-hour trip goin' around, feeding the men one hot meal a day, and then we'd reverse it so we were givin' the last first on the food, so we were livin'

---

[14] The Fiftieth AAA Battalion consisted of four batteries, having two platoons per battery and twenty vehicles per platoon. The mission of the battalion is to serve under an army corps and/or to be assigned to an infantry division, or be assigned to any unit needing extra firepower. The battalion has approximately six hundred men and fifty officers. Small units, such as my platoon, can be assigned to other fighting units, such as Colonel Puller's marines. The twin 40 mm and the quad fifty-caliber machine guns could fire about 240 rounds per minute. The infantry school at Fort Benning, Georgia, had what they called "the mad minute," where every weapon in an infantry division fired out in a zone to the front for sixty seconds. You have to see it to believe. No trees, bushes; not even a blade of grass was left standing. My platoon could have been part of the show of power. [Merrill Harper]

out of the jeep trailer, sleepin' on the ground, and this was late October and November of 1950.

We couldn't find a place to stay or anything, [and] we didn't have any big tents, so one of the guys found this hutment that was empty, and so we moved into there so we could try to set up a stove and warm up the men. My men took a can of diesel up in the second story, and they were heatin' it so the people had a warm place to sleep. I had just gotten up one mornin' 'cause I was gonna let my assistant take the food run. I had just got dressed with my fatigues on, and I had my field jacket handy and my weapon was layin' on the bed, on a cot, and all of a sudden the ceiling just opened up with flaming diesel fuel. It was droppin' all around me and I ran through the side of the hutment to get out alive and not get caught on fire and the whole building just went up in flames. It was so cold that I had to stand about judging the temperature of the heat, close enough to get some heat, but far enough back so I didn't get burnt. The ammunition we had stored in there started goin' off and there was bullets flyin' in every direction. It was something. I didn't have any parka. I didn't have a sleepin' bag 'cause it got burnt up. All my gear I had brought from the States with me burnt up. I had put two fifths of whiskey in my duffle bag to give to the men for Thanksgiving and Christmas, and that all burnt up.

CHAPTER 6

CHESTY PULLER—
MOST DECORATED MARINE

When we got up the next morning, December 13, 1950, we got orders to move out to meet Colonel Puller's marines just south of the Chosin Reservoir. It was a sixty-mile run up the pass. We made the run, and there was snipers all along the way, takin' pot shots at us. We passed several burnt-out vehicles, and finally we came to the ravine in between the mountains there where Colonel Puller had his 150 men. The Chinese was shootin' into the area from quite a distance away. We were under attack, and Colonel Puller says, "Is they anything you can do to stop those Chinese?" I said, "I think I can. Let me take one of my vehicles." (I had the four machine guns on it.) We went down and I says, "Back it up!" And then I climbed on top of it and I told the gunner, "I want you to start in the tall bushes at the bottom and I want you to work your way right and left, up the ravine." It was about a quarter of a mile high and there was enemy fire comin' out all around us, and so he started and he just ate those bushes up with the machine-gun fire. He was killin', and we counted eighty dead Chinese soldiers when we got through, and that cut the incoming fire out immediately. My other vehicles were backing up the one fifty-caliber vehicle [waiting in readiness if called upon to assist in the attack]. Colonel Puller's comment was, "That's purty good for this day!"

The next morning, it's December 14, 1950, minus twenty to minus fifty degrees. A jeep roared up right quick at ten minutes to eight and a lieutenant leaped out and he says, "You're s'posed to cross the IP, initial point of attack, in ten minutes!" (The IP is where I met Colonel Puller and we led the troops into the attack on the south side of Hill 1457.) He says, "The captain got drunk last night and forgot to send anybody up here to tell you!"

I was waitin' on Colonel Puller at eight o'clock on that day, and he wouldn't get in the jeep, so I got out of the jeep. We walked along there, and then the attack started on the south side of Koto-ri Pass, where they was about five hundred Chinese enemy soldiers on the south side. We went up and attacked Koto-ri Pass on the south side, and it was the fiercest fighting I've ever seen. The snow was comin' in and it was swirling around the marines and our troops, and every time you'd get an opening there'd be some Chinese soldiers shootin' at you. I was shootin' back, and everybody was shootin'. And we came up to where the road had been cut into the side of the mountain, and it was about a forty-foot cut and you could see the Chinese at times and every time I did, I'd shoot one of 'em. Colonel Puller never took his gun out. He just walked along and bullets was hittin' 'round us. Why we didn't get hit, I don't know.

All of a sudden I looked up and here come a marine sliding down the side of an embankment. He started staggerin' across the road, and there was about an eight-hundred foot drop and he was fixin' to walk over the edge. He must have weighed a hundred pounds more than I did, and I finally got him turned just enough so that he didn't walk over the edge. He had been hit in the head, and the bullet cut his head all the way around in a circle, and you could almost see his brains where he'd been hit. I got him to set down on this pile of rocks that had been pushed off to the side.

Then I felt better that he had made it so he could get help from the people comin' up behind us [December 14, 1950].

We kept on fightin' all mornin', and that afternoon we finally took all of the south side of Koto-ri Pass, which is about ten miles from the Chosin Reservoir, where the First Marine Division was fighting three hundred thousand Chinese soldiers. I estimate I killed ninety Chinese out of the five hundred Chinese that we encountered on the south side of Koto-ri Pass.

Colonel Puller came over to me, and he said, "On the north side of Koto-ri Pass there's ten thousand Chinese who've set up an ambush. When the First Marine Division comes out, the ten thousand Chinese are gonna disrupt them, and then the three hundred thousand Chinese are gonna circle around 'em and wipe out the whole marine division."

How many men did you have?

I had forty men. Two officers. Two of my men were killed on Koto-ri Pass: the squad leader and the driver.

And how many vehicles?

Eight vehicles. Nine, countin' my jeep and my command vehicle, which was steel plated, all the way around it.

December 14, 1950, the sun came out about noon and my captain who commanded Battery A came up. He had our executive officer, an ordinance lieutenant, and two ordinance soldiers. He had two objectives for me. Initially he says, "I come up to get my Silver Star." I said, "Silver Star?" He says, "Yes. You gonna write me up." Then we were all to proceed up the road to retrieve the bodies of the two American soldiers near our captured half-track. I tried to impress on him the danger this would present, which led to a heated argument.

Two weeks prior, the commanding general of X Corps [Major General Edward M. Almond] had requisitioned one of my quad fifty machine gun vehicles and they was sendin' it to the Chosin Reservoir. In the horseshoe-shaped Koto-ri Pass the Chinese had jumped it, killing my driver and my sergeant who was in charge of the vehicle. Now we could see that vehicle. Actually, the Chinese had that vehicle, and they're not gonna let us go up there.

I assume the captain and his officers wanted us to recapture that vehicle. Now the captain says, "You don't have any guts, do ya?" I says, "I got guts." But I says, "Colonel Puller has told us there's ten thousand Chinese on that side of the mountain and those Chinese have that half-track." "Oh!" he says, "You don't know what you're talkin' about!" I says, "Okay! Follow me!" And I started up through three feet of snow.

I was breakin' the snow as the lead man and we got within about three hundred feet of that half-track. The Chinese had taken the fifty-caliber machine gun off of the vehicle and put it inside of a shepherd's hut where you couldn't see it. And they were back inside. They had also taken the thirty-caliber machine gun off and they had placed it under the vehicle where they could shoot down, straight down the road. They opened up, full fire. I went down and I was afraid they were gonna attack, so I hollered for the captain and nobody answered. I was lookin' for them to charge me and so from one o'clock until it got dark about eight, they shot at me all afternoon, 'cause every time I'd raise my head above the three feet of snow the people on the other mountain could see me, 'cause they were higher than I was.

Ten thousand Chinese were shootin' at me all afternoon. Bullets comin' from all directions and splattered around above my head in the snow. Five bullet fragments hit me in the side of the face but they were from bullets that were spent to where they were out of energy or I'd of been dead. So, I was layin' there in the ice and snow.

I looked up and there were about forty armed Chinese walking up the south slope, almost over my head. They were on their way to attack the marines higher up on the south slope. They were walking single file. I shot the first nine Chinese and I was wounded two times. The rest of the Chinese laid down on the snow and crawled back to their troops. Each Chinese was carrying a heavy backpack. They would have killed a lot of marines. [December 14, 1950]

The Chinese around or in our captured half-track had those two machine guns, with which they kept part of my platoon pinned down. (The platoon was in a covering position to back us up.) The Chinese were shooting three feet on either side of me. Since I was close to the machine guns, I decided to shoot one Chinese at a time, then hide for a minute or two. Then I would pop up and shoot another Chinese. I shot fourteen Chinese soldiers and kept the machine guns and hand grenades from injuring my troops. The medic pulled five bullet fragments out of the left side of my head when I got back to my platoon at 8:00 p.m.

It was about fifty below zero and 'course I had no winter clothes. I was layin' there in nothin' but a field jacket and fatigues and I could feel my feet freezin'. Every time I would look up there was more people shootin' at me. So when it got dark I rolled over into the ditch and it was frozen hard as a rock. I crawled down the ditch for a quarter mile back to my unit. Havin' nothin' to sleep on, my men covered me in two feet of snow for the night and I slept till the next morning under two feet of snow.

Regarding the captain's request for me to recommend him for the Silver Star: About one month after this incident, sometime in January of 1951, the battalion commander, a lieutenant colonel, handed me a yellow pad and a pen and said for me to write up the captain for a Silver Star. I handed the pen and pad back to him, saying, "Sir, I can't do that because I have been taught not to lie." He looked sheepish and instructed me to leave.

CHAPTER 7

HOW TO DEFEAT A TEN-THOUSAND-MAN AMBUSH WITH JUST FOUR MEN

Five o'clock the next mornin', December 15, 1950, Colonel Puller sent for me. My feet felt like they had about a ten-pound block of ice on 'em and I couldn't judge cause I didn't have any feelin'. I reported to Colonel Puller and he says, "The marines are gonna try to break out this afternoon. You gotta take those ten thousand Chinese soldiers off that mountain or run 'em off!"

I got my gunner of the twin 40 mm half-track and I says, "Okay. I have a set of binoculars. I'm gonna be your eyes." Then we worked out a signal for when I wanted him to go right, and they'd relay this to the gunner. So in about thirty minutes the Chinese broke the snow ('cause it had snowed overnight) to take a pee. When they did I told the gunner, I says, "Okay, zero in on that yellow snow." So he did, and we had highly explosive rounds and we had white phosphorus rounds. So I says, "Okay. Let's try 'em with the white phosphorus rounds." And he came within about five feet and he got 'em all.

So then, I worked from that spot and I would shift him either up, down, right, or left, 'cause the Chinese was sittin' in a box,

21

roughly, and so we worked it all day till 2:00 p.m. We were killin' probably about ten Chinese with every round. As we worked up the side of the mountain and across and back, finally about 2:00 p.m., the [Chinese Army's] bugle blew. I counted roughly in terms of fifty, fifty, fifty; hundred, hundred, hundred, that there was only 2,500 Chinese that got off the mountain, so we musta' killed 7,500, which isn't bad for a day's work, when they were tryin' to kill me.

The gunner was in the 40 mm turret and was well protected. The loader was the most exposed person of the crew. He would pop up with a round, place it in the shell receptacle, and pop back down in the turret. The ammo handler would give the loader the correct ammo and duck out of sight. He was standing on the ground behind the tank. I was standing on the ground in front of the vehicle, unprotected. The rest of the men were protected by a half inch of steel most of the time. My other vehicles and men were backing up the twin 40 mm. I got hit in the face about seventeen times with spent bullets that kept comin' in because they were shootin' at me. They knew they were in trouble cause I was wipin' 'em out and that gunner was the best that I'd ever seen.

Between 8:00 a.m. and 2:00 p.m. December 15, 1950, we killed about 7,500 Chinese and ran about 2,500 Chinese over the next mountain, all within six hours. For six hours I stood next to my twin 40 mm gun out in the open with my field glasses so that I could see the ten thousand Chinese and direct the fire for my gunner. At 3:00 p.m. on December 15, 1950, I reported to Colonel Chesty Puller, marine commander, "Sir, mission completed. The ten thousand Chinese who were in ambush have either been killed or run over to the next mountain." Colonel Puller looked at me, with my seventeen wounds, and said, "Harper, you have earned the Medal of Honor." Apparently that Medal of Honor has been lost, as well as the other medals he promised.

CHAPTER 8

FIRST MARINE DIVISION BREAKOUT FROM CHOSIN RESERVOIR

So, about two hours later, December 15, 1950, a couple of marines came around the bend and started goin' up the road past where they was. They slid down the side of the mountain, about a two-hundred-foot drop, then climbed up our side of the hill and reported that they were marchin' out. General Smith commanded the First Marine Division.

O. P. Smith?

O. P. Smith. He had performed one of the miracles of takin' fifteen thousand marines and fightin' three hundred thousand Chinese and not gettin' wiped out. Part of the Seventh Army Division, what was left of it, had staggered in to his unit and they helped them marry up with them. Colonel Puller walked over to me that day [December 15, 1950] and stated, "You earned the:

    a. Medal of Honor for killing 7,500 Chinese troops who had set up an ambush for the First Marine Division, and you ran 2,500 Chinese soldiers over the mountain while being wounded seventeen times. [December 15, 1950]

    b. Navy Cross for singlehandedly stopping forty Chinese from launching a new attack on the marines on the south side of

Koto-ri Pass by killing nine Chinese who were leading the attack while being wounded two times. The rest of the Chinese went back to the north slope of Koto-ri Pass. [December 15, 1950]

c.   Distinguished Service Cross for leading the attack on the south slope of Koto-ri Pass and killing over ninety Chinese of the five hundred Chinese soldiers who were attacking the south pass. [December 14, 1950]

d.   Silver Star for wiping out two machine-gun nests singlehandedly and being wounded five times. [December 15, 1950]

e.   Silver Star for leading an attack on eighty attacking Chinese soldiers and killing all eighty with your machine gun. [December 13, 1950]

f.   Bronze Star for saving one marine who was shot in the head and keeping him from walking off an eight-hundred-foot drop. (I then shot two Chinese soldiers who were chasing the marines.) [December 15, 1950]

Colonel Puller wrote down the above, plus I gave him my name, rank, serial number, and unit so he could write me up for the above battles.

I have waited all these years for my Medal of Honor and other medals from the First Marine Division. Colonel Puller (USMC), First Lieutenant Messenger (USA), and M/Sgt. Hill (USA) were witnesses to the above events. Who do I go to for help on the medals?

So, startin' at six o'clock that night (December 15, 1950), the marines started walkin' out. Sixty miles to the rear, the navy had set up a recovery program to get everybody aboard ships, to get 'em transported out of there. Colonel Puller came over to me and he says, "I want you to be the last person off this mountain. I want you to be the last person off the beach." I says, "Yes, sir!"

And that's the last I saw of Colonel Puller. And he walked out with his marines.

We stayed up three days and three nights. My men and I were awake, defending, ready to defend against those Chinese. We knew there was twenty-five hundred just over the hill. We knew we had three hundred thousand in Chosin that was comin' on both sides of us, that wanted to run a pincer movement around and cut us off and then just chop us up in little pieces.

The first night, a vehicle pulled up and they had wounded marines stacked up just like cordwood. They had, probably, a hundred wounded soldiers in that vehicle and [each of the other vehicles]. I counted thirty-five 2½-ton trucks, was all they had left. The rest of 'em had been destroyed. And the thirty-five 2½-ton trucks had probably a hundred wounded to the vehicle, and they went on through.

And so finally everybody came through and then I gave the orders for my men to infiltrate into the marines so they'd have protection at the end of the convoy. And then I got into the command vehicle. The radio didn't work. It had frozen. We had no way to communicate. We still had been out of food and water this period of time and we had just about eaten up the gallon of cherries. There was one cherry in the morning and one in the night, and that's how we survived, on the moisture from the cherries. Frozen cherries. We'd take a bayonet and pick 'em out [*soft chuckle*]. My driver [had] picked up the gallon can of cherries at a food depot in Pusan before we came up to North Korea.

We started down the mountain, and here's these Chinese that had gone on by us. And they were firing at us from the right and firing at us from the left. Everybody on my vehicles had a machine gun. I had put extra machine guns that wasn't authorized in peacetime on the side of my vehicles. Every man had a machine gun and we were firing right, left, and I had one in the rear. We were catching fire all along there and I was takin' care of shootin' at the Chinese that were shootin' at us from the rear. I must've hit a bunch of 'em 'cause they quit firing for awhile and then we went further down the road traveling at the rate of whatever the marines were walkin', that's how fast we were goin'.

About ten miles down the road we found the thirty-five 2½-ton trucks with the wounded. The Chinese [had run] a pincer movement, killing the thirty-five drivers and then taking the gas cans, pouring the gas on the wounded, then burning all the wounded alive. [Now] no one was alive.

We finally traveled the sixty miles to within five miles of the Songchon River, just beyond Hamhung, and we'd been without sleep for nights and nights and there was an eight-inch howitzer battalion. They permitted us to use their sleepin' bags and cots. Everybody from our battalion was assigned a cot, and they stayed up twenty-four hours to accommodate us, which was very nice. When I laid my head down, I didn' wake up for twenty-four hours.

And, so, we got in our vehicles and then my platoon was assigned rear guard. The Chinese were comin' in down the river, which flowed into the ocean there. They had one bridge that went over that river. That was it. The men went out to this little airfield and found the overcoats that we should've had before we went out to the Chosin Reservoir. They had a stack of 'em about fifteen feet high and about twenty feet long that was just packed up, and a guard was burning the overcoats. Nobody'd made any effort to send them out to the troops that needed 'em. I got all my men and me an overcoat.

So we were sendin' the vehicles up the valleys and we'd shoot the Chinese comin' down to try to just stave 'em off until we could get everybody on board ship. And we were running probably a five mile area that we were just kinda patrolling to try to buffer, put off as long as we could, Chinese closin' on us. Without my platoon, the rest of the Fiftieth AAA Battalion had loaded up and gone on to Pusan without telling me.

The engineers come in and said, "We're gonna blow the bridge at five o'clock tonight. Get across the river." So, we got across the river and we found an old schoolhouse 'cause I didn't know how long we was gonna be there and I needed some way to warm my troops up 'cause it was so cold. We took glass out of some of the windows and we taped the others, and we sealed it up, lit the fire, and then I thought oh, we can bring all the men in, rotate 'em through, and let 'em warm up. As I spoke that, they set the explosives off at the bridge and the explosion just blew out every window in the building. We turned off the fuel and mounted up and went back out to the dike.

They had a big dike that ran across four lanes at the last hill overlooking the river. I said, "Okay. We're gonna set up here." Everybody had a machine gun and we didn't know how many were gonna attack us at one time. I says, "Okay, we have to fight to the finish here 'cause we don't know exactly the number that's comin' and when we can be able to get to the ship."

So, as the night progressed it was blacker than black and you couldn't see anything and when you got down close to the ground you could look out across where the river [was] an' it looked like a moving mass, there was so many Chinese coming. I was waiting and thanks to an engineer captain, he pulled up about 3:45 a.m. and he said, "Don't you know they're gonna blow the docks down at the ships at 4:00 a.m.?" And I says, "Nobody's told us." So he says, "Get on the LST immediately!"

The navy guns were each assigned a grid square to shoot in. This really slowed the three hundred thousand Chinese from overrunning my platoon. The navy really did a great job keeping their grid squares covered with exploding shells.

This was Christmas Day, December 25, 1950. I was the last person to get on the last LST at 3:55 a.m.

27

So we put our guns on the vehicles and everybody took off. The captain of the LST gunned that LST and even before he closed the tailgate we were movin' to get out of the way of everything that was goin' up, and debris had to come down. So I told the men, I says, "Get under the vehicles. There's gonna be cement fallin' and some of it may be the size of an engine, you know."

And sure enough, at four o'clock the docks blew everything and it went up, and there was chunks of cement the size of a chair hitting the vehicles, and fortunately every man was under a vehicle. An' we loaded onto a transport ship and I've never been so glad to see a ship and a navy crew in my life, as I never thought I'd get to see it. They gave us a bed and I slept for twenty-four straight hours.

CHAPTER 9

THE FIFTIETH AAA BATTALION SAILS TO PUSAN

The Fiftieth AAA Battalion sent an advance supply party to Pusan a week before we got on a ship. The X Corps had two boxcars filled with beer on the dock in Pusan. Our men held the MPs up at gunpoint and unloaded the two boxcars of beer and carried it to our staging area thirty miles away, which was on the side of a thousand-acre wheat field. When we pulled in it was a big party going on with beer.

The West Point lieutenant colonel held battalion formation and threatened everyone that the beer was to be put back in a pile by morning. The next morning not even one can of beer could be seen. The lieutenant colonel held another formation and threatened everyone. Then he got in his jeep and left. All the drivers drove their vehicles to the wheat stacks and loaded the cases of beer, which had been hidden within sight of the lieutenant colonel. The lieutenant colonel never knew.

Then, it took us four days to get back to Pusan from Hamhung. At Pusan we were guarding an airfield thirty miles northeast of Pusan and then they moved us to guard Pusan Bay and all the shipping. At that time we were recovering from all of our Chosin Reservoir experience. People were gettin' some sleep and square meals. I had gone from 170 pounds down to 118 pounds. You could see my ribs [*chuckle*].

Our jeep, which we had had since we had been in Korea, only ran in second gear and reverse. We couldn't get it to go in anything else. That night, I heard a vehicle comin' in. The sergeant had wanted to go to town. I walked out the next day and there was almost a brand-new jeep and I says, "Where's the old jeep?" They says, "Well, the MPs picked it up and they took it to the impound lot." I says, "Are you kidding me? Whose jeep is this?" They said, "This is some colonel's who is with an artillery unit." I says, "We can't have this jeep." I says, "They'll catch us."

And so I told 'em, I says, "All right. What we're gonna do, I'm goin' to the impound lot and I'm gonna ask for my vehicle back and in the meantime y'all get rid of this vehicle." So, we went into the MP's station, and I knew I couldn't bluff my way out. I had to just make a truthful statement: that I had written a bunch of letters, the first letters I'd written in two or three months, and I had put them into the jeep's glove compartment.

When I walked up to the MP desk I says, "Do you have my letters?" He says, "You talkin' about this bunch of letters here?" I says, "That's mine!" I says, "Do you have a scrawny old ugly jeep out there that you're ashamed of?" He says, "You must own that jeep that'll only go in second gear and reverse." I says, "Yes, I do." So we went out and got in the jeep. Nobody said anything. We drove out of the MP impound slowly, waitin' for somebody to stop us. And the guys, I don't know what they did with the other jeep. I guess they left it somewhere close to headquarters, where it could be found.

But we stayed there about a week, then we got orders to go up the coast to Inchon, and make another Inchon landing. We loaded up my platoon and our gear on an LST and the Japanese stevedores ran it. The captain was Japanese. We started out and a storm hit us and we went up the Yellow Sea, parallel to the west coast of Korea. We were pitched around just like a toy in the ocean. It was so bad it took us four days and four nights to get up from Pusan to Inchon and it should have taken us about two days. But we made it, fortunately.

CHAPTER 10

THE KIMPO AIR BASE DEFENSE

We landed at Inchon again and at that time my platoon was assigned to defend Kimpo Air Base. Kimpo Air Base was the busiest air base in the world at that time. They had either a plane takin' off or a plane landin' every two minutes. It was somethin' you had to see to believe that anybody could really do that with aircraft. So my platoon set up around the whole airfield and these planes would go up and they'd be shot full of holes when they came back. Some planes would come back on one engine and crash land on the runway, so they decided they needed to put a strip of sand on the side of the runway so they could go into the sand and save the aircraft, which they did, and it saved a B-29 and dozens of other aircraft from destruction.

The defense of Kimpo Air Base was an experience that few people have. The air force security officer, I was talkin' with him and they were losin' equipment. Every night. They could not figure out where the equipment was goin.' Even engines to a jeep was bein' stolen. The guard at the gate said nothin' came through them.

While I was checkin' my guns and gunners, I happened to look out and there was a big circle [manhole cover]. I guess about eight feet in size. It had a piece of new rope stickin' out from

32

[under] it. And I walked over to it and I couldn't [move it]; the top was fastened underneath some way. So I went to the security officer, and I said, "Come with me."

We went out and I said, "I betcha stuff is goin' down this hole." And sure enough, they got a wrecker to come out with a big hoist and they lifted that top off. And the rope ran down into an area underneath the runway. At the north entrance of the runway they had big gates put in and they could back trucks in underneath the runway and they could load and unload all sorts of equipment and nobody would've known it. I just happened to catch it with the rope stickin' out. So they welded it shut. And then they welded the steel doors shut at the north entrance.

Who was stealing it?

The Koreans.

What would they do with it?

Well, they were usin' it for their vehicles. And they were usin' it to trade for stuff that some of their people needed.

CHAPTER 11

GUARDING SUWON AIRFIELD

So after about four months of bein' at Kimpo, my platoon was assigned to go to Suwon Airfield, twenty miles south of there. At Suwon Airfield during World War II, the Japanese had built bunkers for their Zero fighter planes. When my assistant lieutenant and I saw the Zero bunkers, we said they would make a great command post. When we started to walk into the bunker, the ground was covered with wharf rats about eighteen to twenty-two inches long. We both said, "Look for another site."

We got our two-man tent up and I had a sleeping bag with a blanket liner. About 2:00 a.m. the Chinese blew their bugles for an attack on the village about half a mile away. I had turned over in the wool liner but not the sleeping bag. Needless to say, for the next ten to fifteen minutes the bugles got closer, the zippers wouldn't unzip, and complete claustrophobia set in. The Chinese had been bayoneting our soldiers while they were in their sleeping bags. Somehow I got my bag unzipped, got my machine gun, and directed my weapon to fire on the Chinese. We found sixty bodies the next day.

I had a Korean houseboy who spoke some English. He would take our clothes to his mom who washed and starched our clothes. He told me the houseboy at headquarters battery was a bad thief.

I tried to tell the executive officer he needed to watch for this thief. While I was there at headquarters battery they were loading all the battery's blankets into two 2½-ton trucks. The executive officer said the houseboy had a place in Seoul that would try to clean them. I said, "Are you sending a GI guard with him?" He said, "I trust our houseboy." Three days later the battery houseboy still hadn't returned. The military police couldn't find the fake address. The battery commander never saw the battery houseboy or about 150 blankets that were the battery's. The black-market rate was $10 per blanket, or $1,500 total. This was a fortune during the war.

There was a rice paddy next to our command post. Every day an old man, over eighty years old, was hoeing the rice field with a hoe handle about eighteen inches long. I took a broom handle and my houseboy, and we told the old man to let me replace his handle with the long handle so he wouldn't have to lean over and that would help his back from hurting. The old man said okay. For the rest of the day the old man hoed with the long-handled hoe.

The next morning my houseboy said, "Come see the old man." The old Korean man had put his eighteen-inch handle back from the hoe and was bent over, hoeing. I asked my houseboy to ask the old man why he put the eighteen-inch handle back on. The old man looked me in the eye and said this hoe had been good enough for his father, who did it at eighty-eight years old, and the eighteen-inch hoe had been good for his grandfather, and all his older parents before that. And then the old man thanked me for looking after his back, but he had to follow all his parents' customs. So much for progress.

They [Suwon Airfield] had planes flyin' in and out all the time. One plane came in, bounced off the runway, up about forty feet and bounced again thirty feet, bounced again twenty feet, and then it just spun off. We ran out to see what was goin' on, and the pilot was dead. Somehow he got that plane back to the runway, got it down, was able to land it, and somewhere in there he died.

He was the only one on the plane?

Yeah. Stuff like that made you wonder how in the world it can happen. From there we got a call about ten o'clock one night from headquarters and I was told to bring my assistant [lieutenant] and come over. All the officers in the battery, which were seven, were there. All the officers was sittin' there and a deck of cards was on the table. And everybody had one card turned over in front of 'em. And the executive officer, who I outranked, he says, "Cut a card." And I says, "What are we cuttin' the cards for? Are we doin' money, whatever?" He says, "Cut a card. Cut a card." And I teased him. I said, "Well I'm not cuttin' a card until I know what I'm gonna draw." He says, "Cut a card." So I says, "Well, let's see." And I was just playin' along with him, and I says, "I guess that since you've got a queen, I need a card higher than you and I think it'll be an ace." I picked the deck up and I played with the deck a little bit and I says, "Hey! I think it'll be the ace of diamonds!' And when I turned it over, there was the ace of diamonds! Never in this world would I have expected to do anything like that [*chuckles*]. I thought the guy was gonna flip.

Anyway, it was for the first R&R, rest and relaxation trip, to Tokyo for a week. And I got the first one out of the whole battalion. The captain had drawn for his battery and I drew the high card for the first officer to go on R&R. I went to Tokyo, I saw the sights, I ate steaks every day, and looked at the shows. The battalion had told me to bring back two cases of booze. All my stuff I had in my duffle bag, I had to leave in Tokyo so I'd have room to bring back booze 'cause it filled up exactly a duffle bag, for two cases. And that was heavy stuff! So, when I got to Seoul, to Kimpo Air Base, I went to headquarters and they took quite a bit of my booze. Then I saved enough for the battery and the men. And I didn't have a vehicle, and they says, "Hey! Take this vehicle back down to your unit!" There was a vehicle sittin' out there and it had Air Force markin's on it. I says, "Why?"

"Oh, just do it!"

So I got in the vehicle and I drove down and it was about an hour before dark. Drove up to the checkpoint, just havin' a good time, still glowin' over the R&R trip. And all of a sudden, the military police, air police, they drew their weapons! An' I thought, "What in the world's goin' on here?" And they lowered the gate and I heard the siren go off. They says, "Don't move!" And I'm sittin' there wonderin', "What have I done now?" In a minute here come the security police, a full colonel, and they said, "Get out of that jeep!" I got out of the jeep, took my duffle bag, set it beside me.

They said, "Where'd you get this jeep?"

I says, "From my headquarters; I was told to bring it back down here to you."

"How'd you get it?"

I says, "I just drove it down. I didn't get it."

They says, "It was stolen Wednesday night!"

I says, "Wednesday night I was in Tokyo."

"You're lyin'."

I finally says, "Well, I don't have any more to say. Call up my commander." So they put me in another jeep; they took me to security headquarters. We went through an hour of "I don't know! I wasn't there!" And finally the colonel said, "All right. I'm callin' your commander."

I says, "Well! Thank you!" He talked with my commander and then he says, "You were in Tokyo, wasn't you?"

I says, "That's right!" Come to find out, this drunken captain I'd had for a former commander, he's the one that stole the jeep, he was down in a drinkin' contest, but nobody turned him in. Fortunately, they didn't press any charges with me.

CHAPTER 12

RETURN TO KIMPO AIR BASE

We were there for about six months and I got notified that I was bein' transferred to another AAA battalion, anti-aircraft battalion at Kimpo Air Base, so I went back to Kimpo again. They were a unit that had been in Japan. They had sent 'em over just to defend Kimpo Air Base, and since I'd been there before, the captain was real glad to see me. I helped him, you know, where the guns should go and everything, so it was really a great time helpin' them out.

Christmas of 1951 came and our headquarters were located right next to the Australian headquarters, and they had a beautiful bar and rec room where everybody could relax, and the Australian officers invited us over for Christmas Eve. They brought in their British Broadcasting people and they were gonna have it broadcast in Australia, from there. And, they found out I had been in Korea longer than anyone else. Been [there] back in September of 1950.

They says, "Why are you still here?"

I says, "Well, nobody'll come from the States to take my place! [*chuckles*] They thought that was humorous. I talked to 'em and they says, "We want to record you and we'll resend it down to Australia."

I says, "Okay." So I struck up a conversation with this announcer and we must've talked for two hours. 'Bout what all I'd done, where all I'd been, and then they edited it. They took out part of it. I had a very, very nice time and a beautiful meal. So, there was some good times and all the people in Australia heard me.

What year was that?

Nineteen fifty-one.

Nineteen fifty-one.

So, New Year's Day of 1952 the North Koreans had a small plane. We called him "Bed-check Charlie." At bedtime, 'bout nine o'clock every night, he'd get up high and he'd turn off his engine and he'd glide in and he had some old bombs he'd drop on the runway and everybody'd go crazy. So this one particular night, it was about a half moon, and you could see the outline of the plane, 'cause we were stationed right over the runway, and we could see him. He'd come over, he'd turn on his engine at the end of the runway, and then he putter-puttered right on out. He came back and he dropped some bombs on another outfit, next to the Han River. They opened fire on him and everybody in the valley opened fire. I don't know how many guns went off, tryin' to shoot that little plane down. All he did was get down on the ground level and nobody could get their guns depressed that low.

A B-26 was comin' in off a mission and he came in around by Seoul to fly west to Kimpo. All of sudden he got caught in the firefight, and they zeroed in on him and he managed to limp into the base and finally got the firing to stop. I mean once you start firing, everybody throws down their communication equipment and you can't talk to anybody. He says he was in World War II and he says, "I have never been in such a firefight in my life!" He says, "I'm lucky to be alive!" They knocked out one engine in his B-26, put some holes in his aircraft.

Then, in February of 1952 I finally got orders to go back to the States. I was told to go to the Pusan, rather than the Inchon deployment office. They kept you there for three days, three nights, confined you to where you couldn't go anywhere. From there we went to Osaka, Japan. We loaded up on an old transport ship that had just come out of dry dock somewhere where it had been since World War II. It took us thirty-two days to go from Japan to San Francisco. I could've walked faster than that, almost! I spent eighteen months in Korea [September, 1950 to March, 1952].

Got back to San Francisco and as I told everybody in Korea before I left, I says, "I don't care where they send me in the United States, there's no place worse than Korea!" Sure enough, they sent me to Fort Stewart, Georgia, down in the Okefenokee Swamp. I got there and I commanded one of the last black companies in the military before they integrated in 1952. The experiences were unique, truly. From there I went to school at Fort Bliss, Texas, and then the unit transferred to San Pedro, California, where I joined it and commanded another black company and I was the first unit to go on a site within the Los Angeles-Hollywood valley industrial site. And I went on a site on a five-hundred-foot hill in Inglewood, where Inglewood, Hollywood, and LA came together.

About two months later we went out to Death Valley in California, and we shot our weapons, 90 mm, out there in about 120- to 125-degree heat and from ten in the mornin' until four in the afternoon you couldn't shoot because the optical waves would break the heat and it would just go in waves. You couldn't focus on anything.

From there I got transferred back to another school in Fort Bliss, Texas. From there I was sent to Germany by ship. I was a first lieutenant, and all the other officers were full colonels with their wives. The ranking colonel made me pull duty officer in the ship captain's office for nine days until we docked at Southampton, England. We were stopping for three days. I had to stand at the ship's gangplank. The ship's captain came and said, "Why are you pulling duty officer?" I said the ranking colonel ordered me. Just then the ranking colonel and wife, with over a dozen colonels and wives, started down the gangplank. The ship's captain stopped the ranking colonel and told him he was duty officer for the next three days, and told me to go to London for three days. This colonel's wife exploded and said if I was under her husband's command she would get me.

CHAPTER 13

GERMANY

I reported to the Thirty-Second Brigade, Mannheim, Germany. They had thirty-two battalions, and they had a firing range on the Baltic Sea where they shot out over the ocean, and a B-26 would tow a thousand-foot cable with a big fabricated target. He'd go out and do an S and come back. We were twenty miles from the Russian line and every time that plane would come in, Russia would go on full alert. They didn't know what was gonna happen, even though they had seen it happen, you know, every time.

So, I was assigned to the Baltic Sea, to the post there. Todendorf Firing Range, which lies east of Kiel on the Baltic coast in Germany. It was commanded by a lieutenant colonel. The British had two firing ranges and NATO [North Atlantic Treaty Organization] had one. There were six NATO countries that came up and fired. The British fired. We had one. There were thirty-two battalions in the zones. They come up to the British zone in 1952. They had a colonel commandin' the post. He lived in Lubeck [West Germany]. He would drive over occasionally, and I ended up doin' all the work and commandin' the post. So, 'bout two months later they apparently had contacted him to meet the commanding general at the train station while a battalion was firing over the Baltic Sea. The colonel didn't pick up the general, and arrived at the post headquarters two hours late.

The general says, "May I use your office?"

I says, "Go ahead, General." And [*chuckles*] you could hear the general all the way outside. He relieved that lieutenant colonel of his command right on the spot. And he says, "You'll have orders for the States!" He turned around to me and he says, "You're the post commander!" I said, "Yes, sir!" Normally a lieutenant colonel commands a post; I was a captain then. Well, I commanded it for fourteen months before they wanted to send me back to a unit. So, I got to know all the battalions that came through on a rotational basis.

While we were there we traveled to Norway, Sweden, and Denmark. Three of us rode up and went through all of those countries. I had a plane, a new plane every two weeks from the American zone. It was two hundred miles by road to go 'round to Bremerhaven, but straight across, it was a thirty-minute ride in a plane. I had to carry a lot of money at that time, so I had the plane to do that.

I had this pilot, and he said, "Let's go to Paris," and "Let's go to Britain, and Scotland," and wherever else.

I said, "As long as you got permission, let's go." I didn't have a battalion comin' in, so I had an open period. So we flew down the coast and went across the English Channel and set down at London Airport, stayed a day or two, then we went up the west coast of England. We could see Ireland over across the way, then we swung over, and swung back to Glasgow, Scotland, and we came down the bay, and there was an aircraft carrier settin' in the bay. It had big poles stickin' up on the side of the thing to keep planes from landin'. But our little plane, he just went down and touched on the deck to see that he could do it, then we went on down about a hundred feet above the ocean.

Under this huge bridge that spanned an inlet there, next to Glasgow, there was a tourist three-decker. He headed that plane right at that three-decker and last minute, he just picked it up and we went over. You could see people screamin' and hollerin'. Couple of people jumped off the side of the ship [*chuckles*], and then we just went under the bridge, went around and landed. We stayed there about two days and he says, "We need to go." It's about ten o'clock in the mornin'. We caught a cab out to the airport and he rushed in to operations and when he came out, he had a newspaper. On the front page: "Mysterious Plane Flies Under Bridge"! Hadn't happened since World War II.

We got in and we took off. We needed to gas up. We could look at the map and there's a military installation on the southeast edge of England. So there wasn't anything on the runways. Looked like an empty air base, almost. So we touched down and oh, man! Out of nowhere there were people with fifty-caliber machine guns and jeeps aimin' 'em at us! People hollerin', "Get out with your hands up!" Everybody had a pistol pointed at us, and we got out and said, "All we want is some gasoline!" "You're not gonna get it here! You get in this plane and—Why are you here?" We showed 'em our military ID cards and they kept us in interrogation about thirty minutes. Finally the colonel says, "Get off of this base, and I mean now!" I said, "We don't have enough [gasoline] to cross the English Channel."

"Well, that's your problem!"

So we took off, and it was beginnin' to get dark, so we crossed the channel and the nearest place was in Belgium. The pilot says, "Okay!" All we had was a compass to follow, and the heading. He says, "You watch it too 'cause we are leavin' this point." I figured out on the map it would be twenty minutes before we got to the airfield. By that time, it got dark. I mean, you couldn't see a light anywhere. We were just flyin' by the seat of our pants on an azimuth toward that airfield. We heard the engine sputter and we got within sight of the runway. You could see the lights. The engine cut off. So we just glided. That plane glided about fifteen miles and we landed on the runway and they had to bring gasoline out to us. After gassin' up, we spent the night and we decided not to got to Paris. That was one of the things about the place. There was always something happening.

In 1954 they had the worst flood of the century over north Germany. We had a money conversion, you know, where they take it off the black market and get the good money back in circulation. I collected all the money from everybody on the post, and I got in the plane. This plane had just come up from the south, from Stuttgart, and we took off. The plane didn't sound right to me, and we were flyin' along over the water. I mean, every field, everything, only the farmhouses were up on high ground, the big dikes ran across everywhere. I listened to that engine, it just didn't sound right. We were 'bout halfway to Bremerhaven when it sputtered, and the pilot says, "Look for a place to land!"

Well, there was only one farmhouse and all the animals were in a pasture of about ten acres. There was a dike. Anyway, he took that plane and as we were losin' power he brought it in over this barbed-wire fence and he set it down. Cows and goats and sheep and everything just ran on both sides, out of the way. We finally got the plane slowed, he set it up on one wheel, and we did a circle about three times. Fortunately, we didn't hit the house.

Well, the British reported one of their fighters goin' down, thinkin' it was a fighter plane of theirs, and they had people out lookin' for 'em. We finally called the post and got a mechanic to bring oil down, 'cause it didn't check out. When they opened up the oil hole on the side of the engine there was a long straw [dipstick] about this long [twenty-four inches] in the oil hole goin' down. I found out we had stored old oil from the year before. This idiot of a mechanic had taken this old oil, changed the engine oil which was good, and put it [old oil] in there. It

45

just, oh, what a mess. So we finally got it to where it would crank up and I kept lookin' at that little short runway that we had. I stepped it off, it was a hundred steps, about three hundred feet. Hamburg was the closest runway to us. So the pilot says, "What do you want to do?" I says, "Go to Hamburg!" So we checked the engine out several times, to make sure, ramped it up to full speed, put the brakes on, and locked it. So we took the plane and backed it up under the trees. We touched the house with the end of the tail to get as many feet as we could. So we revved it up and that thing got about three feet off the ground. Well, the fence was about four feet. It just was not gettin' power. So we came to the fence and the pilot was goin' to hit the fence, so he just picked it up right quick and lifted it, and as we went over he dropped the nose and the little tail wheel hit the top of the fence. I could hear it goin', and fortunately the wheel turned, otherwise if the fence had drug us, we'd of been down in water.

Well, we staggered along. It took us probably five miles before we got up to five thousand feet and then it began to erratically go over and over, and right before we got to Hamburg, it lost power again. That was it. We floated in. We didn't make the runway but we made the grass around it, which was easy to land on. But man! That was a close one!

On another day I told that lieutenant colonel there, I was s'posed to go to Bremerhaven to take care of business. The colonel bumped me out of it. He said he was goin'. 'Stead of the pilot goin' down on a regular runway next to the ocean, he got in the motor pool, which was empty. He revved this plane up so they could take off. And as they started down through there, the plane did not get any speed, and it hit this post and that plane just turned cartwheel over cartwheel, and then it landed upside down and gas was flowin' down. I grabbed hold of the door and the pilot was all shook up. I got his harness, and I says, "Hold onto the top of the plane, on this support and give me some room!" So we finally got him out. Then we got into the backseat and we had a heck of a time gettin' the colonel out! And finally we held him up enough to where we could undo his harness. The investigators who came up said the plane was 98 percent destroyed, and we had managed to save two people out of it.

CHAPTER 14

AN EASTER SUNDAY WEDDING DAY

So from there, I went to a unit at Kaiserslautern, West Germany. At Kaiserslautern I wrote my girlfriend, who is now my wife, and I says, "We need to either get married or go our ways." And she wrote back and says, "Let's get married." Nineteen fifty-six, April first, was Easter Sunday. April first and Easter Sunday doesn't happen again until 2014, so it was a special day.

So I flew back, got married. She came over. Ever'body sayin' well, you'll be on such a honeymoon! There was no quarters there! Before there was five other quarters. They had moved a whole division into Kaiserslautern while I was in the States. It bumped me behind ever'body else, even though my friend put me in the next day, for me. So, we had nowhere to live and we found a place way out in a little German village and that really was awful.

So then, we came back to the States, and I was the instructor of the ROTC program for the sophomores at Middle Tennessee University, Murfreesboro, Tennessee. That was a nice tour, to work with young people like that.

And from there, I went back to Fort Bliss, Texas, in El Paso, and we formed up a Hawk battalion, which are guided missiles.

We went to Giessen, Germany, on the border next to Russia. We were on alert almost all the time. Then I got promoted to major, and I became the executive officer of the battalion. Since we didn't have an operations officer, I also did that work too. I had a unit in the field all the time, working under as close to wartime conditions as I could make it. And I'd leave at five o'clock in the mornin', go out in the field, work with them all day. I'd come in about seven at night. I'd then go to the office and I'd do about three hours of paperwork so it could be on the colonel's desk for the next mornin'. I'd go home and get maybe four hours' sleep. This went on for months and months and months. Then I got selected over twenty-one West Pointers to be the assistant to G-1 personnel in Heidelberg, which was the headquarters for all of Europe, and it was a prestigious job.

CHAPTER 15

FORT BRAGG TO VIETNAM— PSYCHOLOGICAL WARFARE

After about a year, in 1966, I got orders to go to Vietnam. I had ten days to get my family out of Germany, to get 'em settled, and go to Fort Bragg and pick up a special forces unit. I had a heck of a time findin' a place for the family to live in her hometown, a very small place in Georgia. I bought a house and then the tenants wouldn't move out. And here I am, running out of time; I had to get the family settled and here's this drunken guy, wouldn't get out of bed. So I called his boss in Birmingham, Alabama, and I told him, I said, "You've got a bunch of these sites all over the South." I says, "I'm goin' on television, papers, and everywhere else I can find, and I am going to spread the story 'bout your employee, won't get out of the house." Well, it took 'em two days to do it, but they got him out and I got the family in.

Went to Fort Bragg. Picked up my troops, the special forces unit, and we flew across country in an old plane that had been not kept up 'cause the oil was just leakin' out. It just covered the whole wing. We got into Oklahoma that next day. S'posed to be breakfast, s'posed to be gas. Nothin'. We left out of there and got to San Francisco and I wrote up that pilot and that airline. It all went to the military. That pilot come back and he says, "You can't write me up like this." I says, "You didn't have food for my troops, they haven't eaten in twenty-four hours. Almost thirty hours." And I says, "We been cooped on this plane and that engine, I know, has lost most of its oil. You must be running on dry." And I didn't change all the other stuff I had written.

We were loaded on a ship, and we went to Saigon [Ho Chi Minh City] and we sat out in the bay with about a hundred other ships that had been there. Some of 'em had been there for a year. We sat there, day in and day out, and I noticed a little boat came out every day at 4:00 p.m. So I went down and I says, "What are you doing here?"

He says, "I bring the mail out."

I says, "You got quite a bit of room, don't you?"

He says, "Yeah."

I says, "You mind if we ride with ya?" So I got all of my troops down there and we got in that mail boat, and we got on shore, and he says, "There's no way for you to get to Saigon but by plane."

I says, "Okay." I went down to the airport and I says, "What are you flyin' to Saigon?"

The pilot said, "We've got a mission to get barbed wire for reinforcement of a compound."

I says, "Can we ride with you?"

He says, "If you can hold on and sit on barbed wire, you can go." So we all loaded up on the plane and he says, "Now I wanta tell ya," he says, "we're gonna fly straight up and we're gonna fly across, and at five thousand feet I'm gonna aim the plane at the runway to escape fire." He says, "We're gonna get a lot of fire, but we've found that's the best way to avoid it." Sure enough, he did just what he said. Man, I'm tellin' you, we went up and then your stomach would go right straight down and you could see the traces just comin' up by us, 'cause they had the airport surrounded.

And we got in and I'm tryin' to find somebody to get a ride with and I finally found an MP outfit. I says, "We need to go to the Sixth Psychological Battalion." I was to command all the troops, with the troops I brought in.

So he said, "Your unit got bombed out last night. Forty-seven of your men are in the hospital."

I says, "What?"

He said, "The Vietcong put a big wide board across from one building to the other and in the building you were to be sleepin' in, they put shape charges on the roof, and they blew the roof right down on your men."

So, when I got there, it was just a bombed-out buildin'. Forty-seven men in the hospital, the rest of 'em was staggerin' around in shock, and we had no place to go. So, the balcony didn't get blown out. It was salvageable, so I had the men sleep on the floor in the balcony. We had no place else to go. And we, I looked for days, and nobody wanted us around, so I finally asked 'em, I says, "Why don't you want us?"

"'Cause you're number one on the Vietcong's hit list!"

'Cause of our psychological program of makin' up leaflets and dropping 'em over all of Vietnam, and [conducting] speakin' missions. We'd go in ahead of the B-52s and say, "If you don't get out of here, we're gonna bomb you." So that was my job.

So we had the battery commanders there. They'd tell us, the lieutenant colonel and me, "Well, we can't do this, we can't fly this mission, we can't go after midnight." You know. So I told the colonel, "I'm gonna run all these missions myself. I'm gonna go out there and see what the problems are." So during my year in Vietnam, I flew forty-four combat missions troubleshootin' to see why these battery commanders couldn't do what they should have. I corrected it all, and I'd fly missions from midnight till five o'clock in the morning. I'd go out during the daytime, afternoons, and I flew from one end of Vietnam to the other. I flew one mission along the DMZ where the SAM [surface-to-air] missiles were pointed over us. They were shootin' at us with SAM missiles and we were sittin' inside the cone. The cone was five thousand feet, 'cause the SAM missiles couldn't depress any more, and when they'd fire at you it just went right over your head. You could see it takin' off at you, and it looked like it was flyin' right toward the middle of the plane. Just miss us by a few hundred feet. That was one scary mission.

Then we flew all the way across the edge of where the DMZ was between North and South Vietnam, and then we'd turn around and come back and everybody on the ground that had a weapon was firin' at us. 'Bout halfway back I heard it go *rip* and the plane we was in, a little Bird Dog, it had an engine in the front and an engine in the rear. They'd shot out the rear engine. Fortunately, we had one engine to get back in. We had a bunch of bullet holes in the plane. So we got back to the airfield.

So, when we completed that, I came back to Palmdale, California, where there was a Nike missile battalion set up along the mountains overlookin' LA and Hollywood. After about two weeks there, the colonel called me in, and my wife. He had said, "Bring your wife and your children." Which we did, and he says, "You're out of uniform!"

I looked at him, and all the staff was there. He had these shiny lieutenant colonel leaves. My wife put one on me and he put on the other, and I got promoted to lieutenant colonel.

The personnel officer says, "You can either go to Colorado Springs or you can stay here in San Pedro." He says, "Okay. You got twenty-four hours to decide."

Well, my son had an asthma attack, so we rushed him to the surgeon at Edwards Air Force Base, California. The surgeon says, "Try the low humidity in Colorado." He says, "There's a fifty-fifty chance he'll grow out of it."

And we said, "That's the only decision we can make." Even though we wanted to stay in California.

What year was that?

Nineteen sixty-seven.

Nineteen sixty-seven.

We had the movers come. The phone rang. The personnel officer says, "Don't answer the phone! The general's gonna call ya in five minutes and he's gonna demand you stay here!" 'Cause I had a lot of operational experience. He says, "He wants you for operations officer."

I says, "Okay." So sure enough, five minutes later the phone rang. I let it ring. Walked out the door, locked it. Got in the car and we came to Colorado Springs, and that was 1968. I spent three years as Operations Officer of all the United States and Canada and retired in April of 1970.

CHAPTER 16

COLORADO—MOVING INTO THE MOUNTAINS WITH NORAD

Where were you stationed in Colorado Springs?

Old Ent Air Force Base, which is [now] the Olympic Training Center. They tore all the base down. Turned it over to the Olympic Training Center.

So you retired in 1970?

Right. Part of my job back then as operations officer was to run a simulated war drill every three months, and those buildings were just that old wooden construction. I had been trained to be a nuclear warfare officer and I knew if a [an atomic] bomb dropped, the blast goes out like this and then it sucks everything in, comin' back out, and those buildings would just disappear. So I wrote up a paper and sent it in to the colonel. The colonel apparently took it to the general. What I proposed was that we move into Cheyenne Mountain with NORAD and have a console and then we could see the whole picture that they saw, worldwide. And then we could see all of the United States, which we were responsible for. And if a bomb dropped, we'd have that protection. And we wouldn't be sittin' out here, blown away.

Well. They sent my paper to Washington and less than thirty days later they approved it, and the general says, "Get that officer, whoever submitted it. Let him do the work." [*chuckle*] That was me. So I got everything communication-wise, all of the nuts and bolts it takes to move into the Cheyenne Mountain with the air force, and I ran a mission and it went so good it even surprised me. All the generals were slappin' each other on the back and tellin' my commander what a great job I did! [*chuckle*] But I had a lot of fun. A lot of good experience. I met a lot of great people in twenty-two years in the military.

You were in the army all of that time?

Yeah.

But you brushed elbows with a lot of different branches of the service.

Oh, yeah. Marines, air force, navy; so many army units.

Well, there were about three marine units that pulled into Inchon to start with in Korea, weren't there? First, Seventh, and the Fifth?

Yeah. They went just ahead of me there.

And you were in the Seventh Army?

Eighth Army.

Eighth Army. Well, I'm amazed how many experiences you've had . . . or survived.

A higher power has to have some angels out there somewhere helpin' you.

It would seem so to me.

I believed in it.

Well . . .

And I'll tell ya, it strengthens your faith when you go through the baptism of fire and you're lookin' down the gun barrel of all these people and you can see the bullets comin' almost straight at you.

I would think so.

'Specially in an airplane where every third round is an incendiary round, which lights up as it comes, and flyin' in a plane, where we had the open door to push the leaflets out, those rounds at night would seem like they were comin' straight in that door. And they'd miss that plane, or they'd take a piece off of it and the plane would be just inches away from bein' shot down.

So what kind of faith did you have or did the men have that got you through Korea, Vietnam, and all these places?

Bein' wounded twenty-four times, and hundreds of bullets cutting my uniforms to shreds, I have wondered, *Why was I spared?* I have always believed in God and I pray. I remember two nights before the Inchon landing, I couldn't sleep at two o'clock that morning, so I went up on the deck in the light of a full moon and I prayed: *Lord, if you spare my life I want to marry my girlfriend, Jule, and have two children.* After knowing my wife sixty-one years and having a girl and a boy, the Lord has answered my prayer. Our daughter, Julie, fifty-one years old, just died after having cancer for fifteen years (1995–2010). My wife, Jule, died March 4, 2011 (1926–2011). I have cancer from exposure to Agent Orange while flying forty-four combat missions in Vietnam as a psychological operations speaker operator. (We broadcasted audio messages from tapes that warned the South Vietnamese people to go to a safe area that we defined, and for the North Vietnamese soldiers to surrender.)

Well, I think I've always believed, and I think the men, they believed in themselves. And those thirty-three felons turned out to be the best soldiers I had, 'cause they did not sit around waitin' for somebody to look after them. They'd go by a farmhouse and they'd get a chicken with a chicken crate. They'd put it on the back of the vehicle, and they'd go down the road and they'd get another chicken or two. They'd have about eight or ten chickens in there, layin' eggs, and they'd have eggs for breakfast. They looked after themselves, and I guess when you look back on it, they were more innovative as soldiers than if you had taken a group of non-felons and they'd've probably been waitin' for somebody to look after 'em.

Wrapping up, the epigraph found at the beginning of this book not only lends itself to the world situation as it existed at the beginning of the Korean War. It also fits in 2011, fifty-eight years hence from the signing of the cease-fire, July 27, 1953.

> And when ye shall hear of wars and rumours of wars, be ye not troubled: for such things must needs be; but the end shall not be yet. For nation shall rise against nation, and kingdom against kingdom: and there shall be earthquakes in diverse places, and there shall be famines and troubles: these are the beginnings of sorrows.
>
> —Mark 13:7–8
> (King James version of the Holy Bible)